LEMONY SNICKET'S
A SERIES OF
UNFORTUNATE
EVENTS™

BEHIND THE SCENES

WITH COUNT OLAF

LEMONY SNICKET'S
A SERIES OF
UNFORTUNATE EVENTS™

BEHIND THE SCENES WITH COUNT OLAF

EGMONT

EGMONT

A CIP catalogue record for this title is available from the British Library
ISBN 1 4052 1727 8
❖
www.egmont.co.uk

PARAMOUNT PICTURES AND DREAMWORKS PICTURES PRESENT A PARKES/MACDONALD PRODUCTION
A NICKELODEON MOVIES PRODUCTION A BRAD SILBERLING FILM JIM CARREY   JUDE LAW AS THE VOICE OF LEMONY SNICKET
"LEMONY SNICKET'S A SERIES OF UNFORTUNATE EVENTS"   LIAM AIKEN EMILY BROWNING TIMOTHY SPALL CATHERINE O'HARA BILLY CONNOLLY
CEDRIC THE ENTERTAINER LUIS GUZMAN JENNIFER COOLIDGE AND MERYL STREEP   SPECIAL VISUAL EFFECTS AND ANIMATION BY INDUSTRIAL LIGHT & MAGIC   MUSIC BY THOMAS NEWMAN
CO-PRODUCER SCOTT AVERSANO   COSTUMES DESIGNER BY COLLEEN ATWOOD   EDITED BY DYLAN TICHENOR, A.C.E.   PRODUCTION DESIGNER RICK HEINRICHS   DIRECTOR OF PHOTOGRAPHY EMMANUEL LUBEZKI, ASC, AMC
EXECUTIVE PRODUCERS SCOTT RUDIN BARRY SONNENFELD   EXECUTIVE PRODUCERS ALBIE HECHT JULIA PISTOR   PRODUCED BY WALTER F. PARKES LAURIE MACDONALD JIM VAN WYCK
BASED ON THE BOOKS "THE BAD BEGINNING" "THE REPTILE ROOM" AND "THE WIDE WINDOW" BY LEMONY SNICKET   SCREENPLAY BY ROBERT GORDON   DIRECTED BY BRAD SILBERLING

 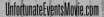

UnfortunateEventsMovie.com

Every so often, a movie captures the imagination

of a generation. Such is the case with LEMONY SNICKET'S A SERIES OF UNFORTUNATE EVENTS. Never before has such a talented cast, crew, and production team joined forces to bring so touching a vision of sibling affection and loss to the silver screen. The Baudelaire childre bark on an odyssey whose scope is reminiscent of the stir -tures of D. W. Griffiths. We are le children's j

Perhaps once every century, someone truly dashing completely changes the way movies are made, orphans are orphaned, and heartthrobs throb. Such is the case with Count Olaf—or, as I refer to him, me!

You might think it's easy to write, produce, direct, design, film, and star in the Greatest Movie Ever Made. Well, let me tell you something: It is if you're Count Olaf! This movie has been my life ever since my last plot was foiled. It's been a long road, filled with sushi, white limousines, free money, and Hollywood hobnobbing. From day one, I stayed true to my vision, which was to become extremely rich!

If you haven't seen my movie, you should put down this book at once, steal a car, drive to the movie theater, and prepare for sheer bedazzlement! This movie has everything, including close-ups of my face!

As Count Olaf, I would like to welcome you behind the scenes of my major motion picture. You may have the urge to pause every few pages and write me a fan letter. Don't resist! I love mail, especially when a check is enclosed!

Of course you may have my autograph!

Count Olaf

THE CAST

Count Olaf..*Yours Truly!* ~~Jim Carrey~~

Violet Baudelaire..*Extra* ~~Emily Browning~~

Klaus Baudelaire..*Extra* ~~Liam Aiken~~

Sunny Baudelaire................*Monkey* ~~Kara Hoffman & Shelby Hoffman~~

Mr. Poe..*Extra* ~~Timothy Spall~~

Dr. Monty Montgomery..*Extra* ~~Billy Connolly~~

Aunt Josephine Anwhistle.....................................*Extra* ~~Meryl Streep~~

Justice Strauss..*Extra* ~~Catherine O'Hara~~

Hook-Handed Man..*Himself* ~~Jamie Harris~~

Person of Indeterminate Gender...........................*Itself* ~~Craig Ferguson~~

Bald-Headed Man...*Himself* ~~Luis Guzman~~

White-Faced Woman #1..*Herself* ~~Jennifer Coolidge~~

White-Faced Woman #2..*Herself* ~~Jane Adams~~

Constable...*Extra* ~~Cedric the Entertainer~~

~~Voice of Lemony Snicket.................................Jude Law~~

Lemony Cricket?? Never heard of him.

APPLY TWO COATS OF WHITE PAINT HERE.

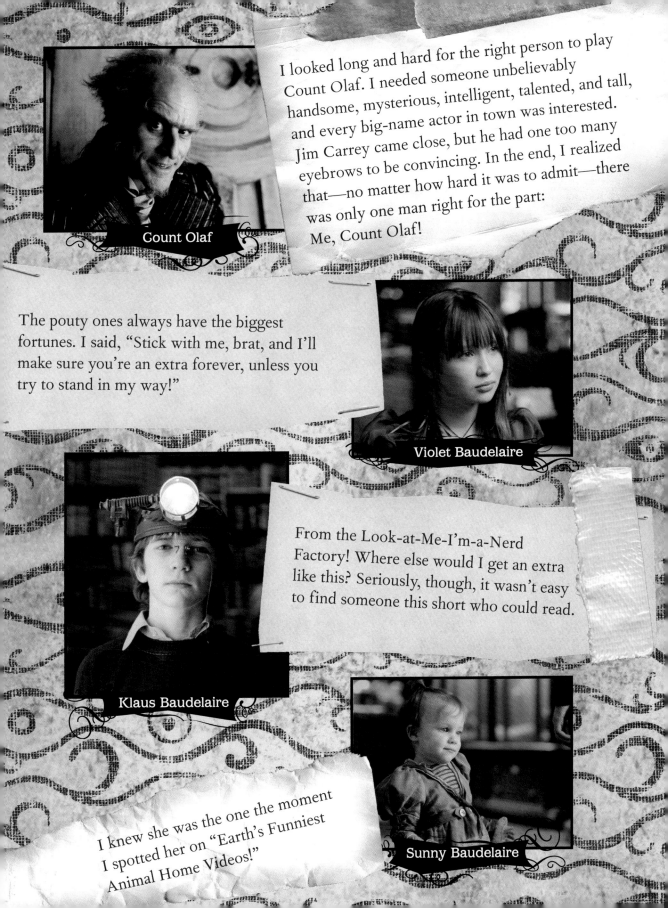

Count Olaf

I looked long and hard for the right person to play Count Olaf. I needed someone unbelievably handsome, mysterious, intelligent, talented, and tall, and every big-name actor in town was interested. Jim Carrey came close, but he had one too many eyebrows to be convincing. In the end, I realized that—no matter how hard it was to admit—there was only one man right for the part: Me, Count Olaf!

The pouty ones always have the biggest fortunes. I said, "Stick with me, brat, and I'll make sure you're an extra forever, unless you try to stand in my way!"

Violet Baudelaire

From the Look-at-Me-I'm-a-Nerd Factory! Where else would I get an extra like this? Seriously, though, it wasn't easy to find someone this short who could read.

Klaus Baudelaire

I knew she was the one the moment I spotted her on "Earth's Funniest Animal Home Videos!"

Sunny Baudelaire

Lemony Snicket

Who the heck put this here??? I have absolutely *no* idea who this is supposed to be. I'll tell you one thing though: he didn't have a part in my movie!!! Move on!

England. No . . . that's not it . . . Britain! I got him from Britain. Apparently, he's a real big extra over there.

Mr. Poe

People thought this extra was really funny . . . funny-LOOKING!!! He sure was susceptible to poison, though.

Uncle Monty

Can't remember where this extra came from. If you think it was easy to act attracted to her, however, you are wrong with a capital R! It's not like she was Meryl Streep or anything!

Aunt Josephine

Bad News on Briny Beach

While playing upon Briny Beach one gray day, Violet Baudelaire, age 14, Klaus Baudelaire, age 12, and Sunny Baudelaire, an infant, are informed by Mr. Poe, a family friend, that their parents have perished in a terrible fire.

No no no no no! No, I say! What kind of opening is this? Please! It's so *dreary*. Skip it! Go directly to my Entrance!

Back to the Baudelaire Ruins

Overcome by shock and disbelief, the children wander through the smoking remains of their beloved familial home.

Well, not as good as my Entrance, but I must admit it was a SPECTACULAR fire!! But no time to gloat. The Baudelaires must be off to their guardian's home to begin anew!

SPOTLIGHT ON ~~A SERIES OF UNFORTUNATE EVENTS: The Books!~~

Me, when I played the
Queen of England.

MASTER OF *Hypnotism*

THE WORLD RENOWNED

COUNT OLAF

HIS UNSURPASSED MAS...
THROUGH...

Relax completely. Deeper.
Deeper still. Let your mind
go. Whenever you see the
word "the," you will write
me a check.

Me, shortly after I
invented fire juggling.

book, THE BAD...
Since then...
...ans have...
...e sold ove...
...ntries. The...met...
...continent are riveted by th...
...and the evil Count Olaf.

Olaf
the Juggler

Oh, come on! Can you spell B-O-R-R-I-N-G? Have I mentioned that my Entrance is coming any second?

The children meet the kindly Justice Strauss and share a moment of hopefulness—until they realize their new home is the run-down house across the way.

Bravo!!! Bravissimo!!! Hurrah!! What presence, what magnetism! Behold, my eyebrow!!! If I may be so bald, this is the first moment of True Greatness in the Greatest Film Ever Made!!

The children arrive at the home of their new guardian, the actor Count Olaf. It quickly becomes clear that Count Olaf is vile, treacherous, and interested in only one thing: getting his hands on the vast Baudelaire fortune!

SPOTLIGHT ON... COSTUMES!

Blending contemporary, Victorian, and Gothic ~~winning costume designer Colleen Atwood se~~ colors, textures, and fashionable lines. Th~~ that transcends time or place. From complicat~~ greatcoats, this film's costumes are a very for~~

Any wolf in sheep's clothing will tell you that nothing ruins a good scheme like a bad costume. That's why I insisted on personally designing every stitch of clothing in my movie! Unfortunately, I was prevented from sewing by a hangna on my left pinky. Thank goodness for m assistant, Colleen Atwood!

Of course, Count Olaf's costumes were the best looking *and* the easiest to design, because I am so good-looking.

Dashing!

Costumes by Colleen Atwood

Count Olaf

Count Olaf

Smashing!

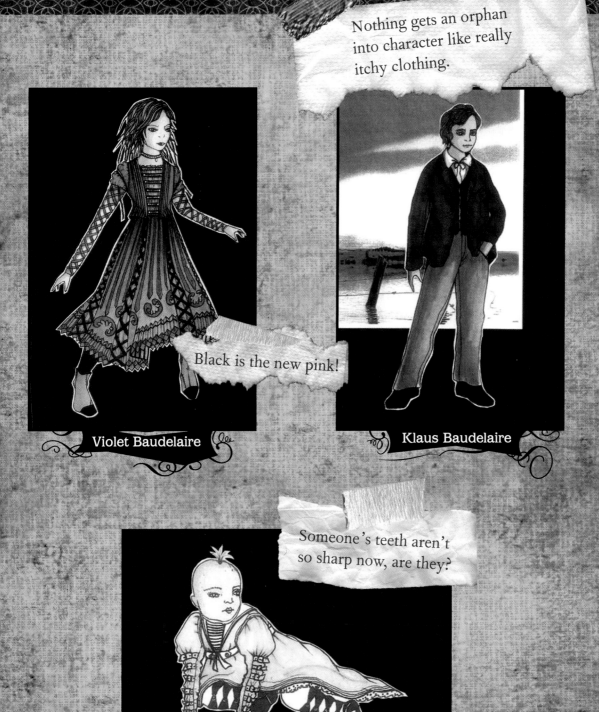

Nothing gets an orphan into character like really itchy clothing.

Black is the new pink!

Violet Baudelaire

Klaus Baudelaire

Someone's teeth aren't so sharp now, are they?

Sunny Baudelaire

It's a Hard-Knock Life

Life in Count Olaf's house is filled with hardship and cruelty. Forced to obey their new guardian's every whim, the orphans face an endless series of back-breaking chores.

Although they were very poor help around the house—the bookworm was constantly whining about the fumes—I am nonetheless quite fond of the scenes of them engaged in hard labor.

Enter the Troupe

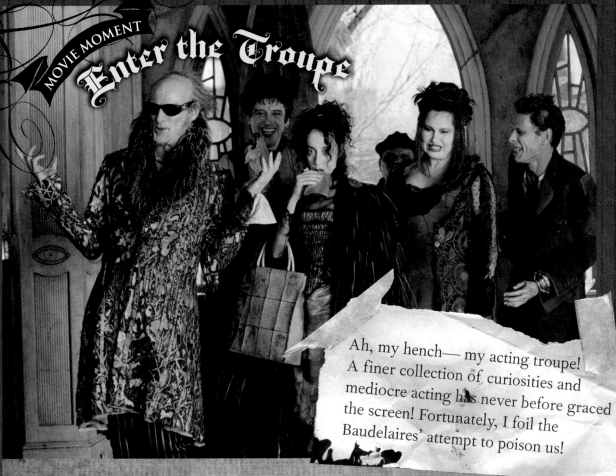

Ah, my hench— my acting troupe! A finer collection of curiosities and mediocre acting has never before graced the screen! Fortunately, I foil the Baudelaires' attempt to poison us!

Count Olaf's theatrical troupe of villainous associates arrives, and Olaf commands the children to cook them dinner while they prepare for an upcoming play.

On the Wrong Track

I always thought it should have ended here, with a big train crash, but the studio just couldn't sell a movie this short. The children are then taken away from me, their rightful guardian, simply because I chose a bad parking space! Is there no justice? I vow that I will always be there for them, and never abandon them to the cruel world!

Count Olaf leaves the children trapped in the path of an oncoming train! Violet struggles to invent something to save them, but the fact that they survive is a miracle and a mystery. Afterward, Mr. Poe removes the orphans from Count Olaf's care, although he fails to see the truly dastardly nature of the villain's plot.

The Baudelaire children go to live with their uncle Monty, a renowned snake expert with a big heart. For perhaps the first time since the death of their parents, the Baudelaires feel safe.

Imagine! Letting little, helpless children play with snakes! The studio said I had to cut these scenes, but I said we *must* keep them in. THIS IS REALITY, I said! This i how cruel and careless some people can be with children!!

A Suspicious Assistant Arrives

Shortly before the children are to accompany Uncle Monty on a research trip to Peru, their brief period of happiness abruptly ends. Stephano, a suspicious new assistant for Uncle Monty, arrives—and the Baudelaires are sure he's up to no good!

A mysterious and dashing assistant appears, just as the children are to be abducted across state lines. Another Moment of Greatness in the Greatest Film Ever Made!

SPOTLIGHT ON... SETS!

Under the careful eye of production designer Rick Heinrichs, a team of visionaries created a world of unusual perspectives and eerie elegance. Filled with places and spaces that are both strangely familiar and alarmingly unknown, the motion picture's extraordinary sets keep us, like the Baude̶̶̶̶ ̶̶̶̶children, guessing about where we are and what lies around every̶̶̶̶

It is truly amazing what a genius like me can create using nothing more than a hammer, a glue gun, and a can of black spray paint. Not since Michael Angelo painted the roof of the Saltine Chapel has the world seen such craftsmanship! Of course, I didn't do it alone—Rick Heinrichs held my ladder.

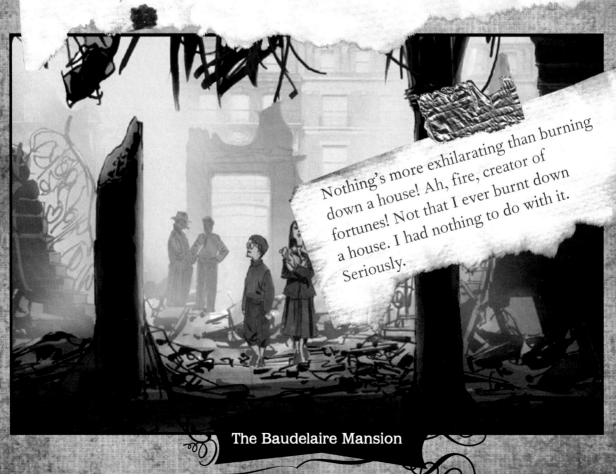

Nothing's more exhilarating than burning down a house! Ah, fire, creator of fortunes! Not that I ever burnt down a house. I had nothing to do with it. Seriously.

The Baudelaire Mansion

Home is where the heartless is! Over 900 eyes and 300 images of me were used to create this set. Unfortunately, budget constraints forced me to make this house much smaller, shabbier, smellier, grubbier, moldier, and dingier than my real-life Count's manor.

Count Olaf's House

What's that supposed to be, a bush?? Can't we even use real giant snakes???

Wrong, wrong, wrong! Where are the snakes? This is supposed to be the Reptile Room!

Uncle Monty's House

For Lake Lachrymose, I wanted a really, really, really big lake. Lake Winnipeg? Not big enough. Lake Superior? Too small. So I got to work with a garden hose. Six weeks later, I had the biggest manmade body of water ever, unless you want to get technical about it.

Lake Lachrymose

What a window! Absolutely perfect for an extra to jump out of!

Aunt Josephine's House

See? See what I said about playing with snakes?! Poor Uncle Monty. He was such a good extra.

Uncle Monty is found dead, poisoned by one of his beloved snakes. Or was he? Stephano and the suspicious Dr. Lucafont are about to escape with the orphans when Sunny proves to Mr. Poe and the Constable that things are not as they seem. Stephano flees!

Yet Another New Guardian

Don't worry. This part doesn't last long!

Arriving at a house precariously perched over Lake Lachrymose, the Baudelaire children are thrust into the care of their aunt Josephine Anwhistle, a widow who is afraid of nearly everything and passionate about only one thing: grammar.

Captain Sham Comes Ashore

Yet another Moment of sheer Greatnessitude! That peg leg sure did chafe, though. But no matter! The show must go on!

During a trip to the market, a suspicious peg-legged sailor appears and sweeps Aunt Josephine off her feet.

SPOTLIGHT ON... COUNT OLAF'S TROUPE!

Very talented!

Some of today's greatest living actors from around the world came together to bring Count Olaf's deranged band of merry sc̶o̶u̶n̶... ing sh̶ould

I don't really think they need *a whole page*. I mean, you just saw a picture of them like ten pages ago! Isn't that enough? I taught them everything they know anyway. Who was bald first? That's right! Me! Who had a white face first? Me and me! Who had hook-hands first? Me again! Who was the first person of indeterminate gender? Me! I mean, not me! I mean . . . never mind.

Another Guardian Gone

Yet again, the unimaginable happens. Aunt Josephine jumps out the wide window to her death, leaving behind a grammatically incorrect note that places the children in the care of Captain Sham.

Crazed by unrequited love for the hunkish sailor, Josephine jumps out the window and leaves him the brats. If only the extra had stuck to the script, we could have ended the movie right here!

Disaster Blows In

With the orphans trapped inside, Aunt Josephine's house is hit by a hurricane and begins to break apart, forcing the children to scramble for their lives as things explode around them. Only an invention of Violet's keeps them all from tumbling into the depths of Lake Lachrymose!

Such violence! Such destruction!! Such terror!!! *This* is what the movies are all about!!! My only regret is that no one was hurt!

SPOTLIGHT ON... PROPS!

A group of elite artisans applied extraordinary attention to detail to every aspect of the Baudelaires' world. Nowhere was this more apparent than in the on-screen inventions of Violet Baudelaire, the greatest fourteen-year-old inventor the world has ever known. A multidisciplinary team of designers and engineers spent thousands of hours bringing Violet's mechanical wonders whirring to life.

It was really hard choosing pieces of wood that would hold up Aunt Josephine's house, but then break when the wind blew.

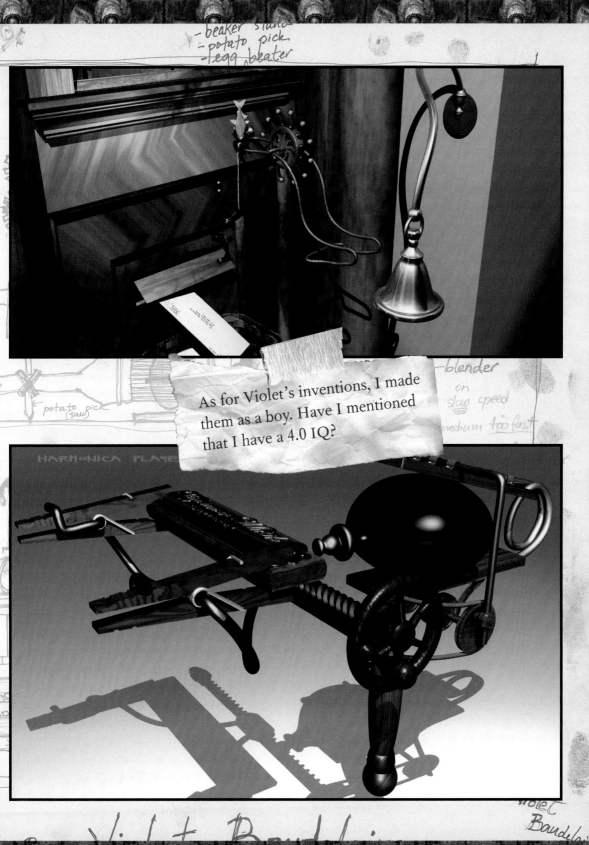

As for Violet's inventions, I made them as a boy. Have I mentioned that I have a 4.0 IQ?

In Hiding

Oh, hooray! Yippee! Aunt Josephine's not dead! Yet.

The children bravely set off to find Aunt Josephine—alive and well! To their dismay, however, she's too scared to leave her hiding place and reveal Count Olaf's plot to the authorities.

The Lachrymose Leeches Attack

What suckers! Also, those Leeches are ferocious!

Klaus cleverly convinces the children's guardian to return with them. Unfortunately, they are attacked on the way by the dreaded Lachrymose Leeches!

SPOTLIGHT ON... THE DIRECTOR!

Acclaimed director Brad Silberling combines epic scope and stirring emotion to bring the world of Lemony Snicket to life, and the result is an otherworldly delight. Mr. Silberling's films, including CASPER, CITY OF ANGELS, and MOONLIGHT MILE, have always taken us to places and introduced us to characters that make the power of love and loss newly familiar. LEMONY SNICKET'S A SERIES OF UNFORTUNATE EVENTS is no exception.

Being a director is a lot like being an evil genius. You tell people what to do, and they do it! Extra, stand over there! Camera guy, get me a Slushee!

Of course, I couldn't do it all by myself. I had people like this kid—my second assistant director, Brad Silberling. I left him in charge of the set for five minutes, and it burnt to the ground! I wish all my henchmen were that talented.

Saved?

Now is one of those times when you might want to write me a fan letter! Our hero reappears to rescue the children, while another extra is lost to the noble art of filmmaking.

Violet devises a signaling device, attracting a nearby sailor . . . Count Olaf! The ruthless villain takes the children and leaves Aunt Josephine to the mercy of the Lachrymose Leeches.

The Perilous Play

The children returned to his care, Olaf hatches his most outrageous and treacherous plot yet: a play whose real-life conclusion will give him control of the Baudelaire fortune!

Pure genius!!!

Baby Sunny is imprisoned in a cage hung from his mansion's mysterious tower, and Olaf makes it clear that she will be dropped to her doom if Violet doesn't cooperate.

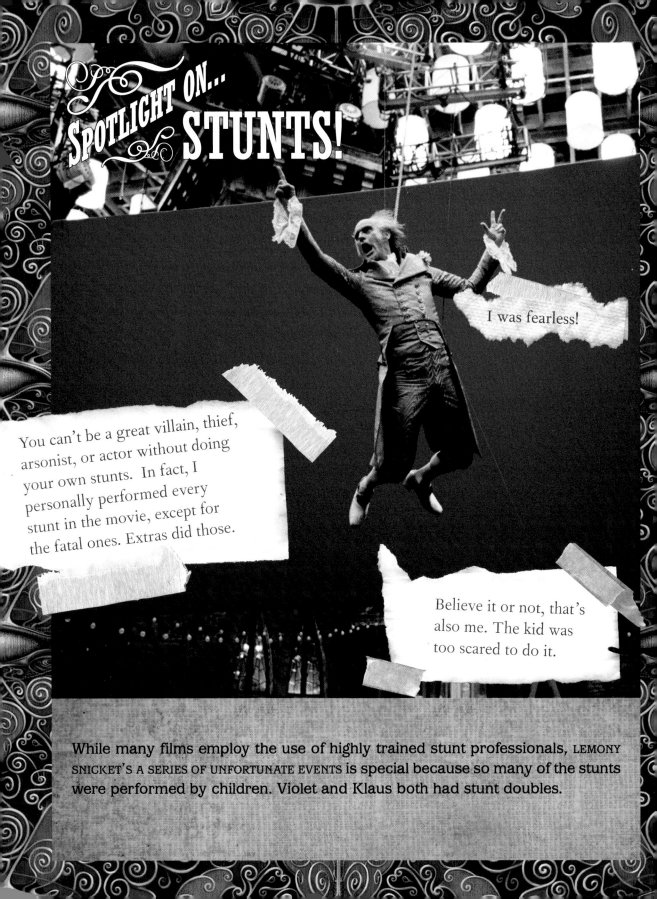

SPOTLIGHT ON... STUNTS!

I was fearless!

You can't be a great villain, thief, arsonist, or actor without doing your own stunts. In fact, I personally performed every stunt in the movie, except for the fatal ones. Extras did those.

Believe it or not, that's also me. The kid was too scared to do it.

While many films employ the use of highly trained stunt professionals, LEMONY SNICKET'S A SERIES OF UNFORTUNATE EVENTS is special because so many of the stunts were performed by children. Violet and Klaus both had stunt doubles.

Klaus to the Rescue

You really think I'd leave a baby in a cage so poorly guarded? Please. Don't be ridiculous. I'm offended. Really.

As Olaf's play unfolds, Klaus slips away to rescue his baby sister. He barely succeeds—but not before noticing that the tower's eye-shaped window is a giant magnifying glass, perfect for starting fires.

MOVIE MOMENT

The Plot Is Foiled

Unfortunately, the children are too late! Violet has already signed over the rights to the Baudelaire fortune, and all hope is lost. . . . But then, from the tower high above, Klaus uses what he's learned to outwit the villain. Count Olaf's scheme is undone!!!

WHAT?! No no no. Absolutely not! This was <u>NOT</u> in the script, and it should <u>NOT</u> be in my movie. I want you to turn the page right now. Go on. Turn it. Do it!! TURN THE PAGE!!!

TURN THE PAGE!!!! NOW!!!!!!!!!!!!!!!!!!

SPOTLIGHT ON... LEMONY SNICKET!

HAVE YOU LEARNED NOTHING???

One mysterious man bears compassionate witness to the fate of the Baudelaires, chronicling every unfortunate event that befalls them. His motiva-tio... ...relationship to th... ...hero's connection to

SNICKET, SCHMICKET! HE DOESN'T MATTER. HE'S WASHED UP. HE'S A LOSER. HE'S USE-LESS. HE'S A FAKE. HE'S A LIAR. HE DOESN'T KNOW ANYTHING. HE IS NOT INTERESTING. HE WEARS A CHEAP HAT. HE'S BORRING!

Have you seen this picture of Captain Sham?

NOW TURN THE PAGE . . . OR ELSE!!!

Olaf Escapes

Once again, Count Olaf escapes! It seems as if justice will never be done, and the children will never find peace.

That's better! Ah, my glorious, theatrical, climactic exit!! Absolutely no special effects or visible wires were used in the making of this scene!!!